in a time of dragons

brittney rittof

Presentation by *BookLeaf Publishing*

Web: www.bookleafpub.com

E-mail: info@bookleafpub.com

ISBN: 9789360948450

First edition 2024

to my Bitsy;

don't ever forget

to stand up

for what's right

ACKNOWLEDGEMENT

i'd like to acknowledge my husband;
without him, i never would have gained
the courage to step out of my comfort zone
and to step up to my potential

PREFACE

this started as a simple project i wanted to
partake in. in the end, this turned into a piece
that i needed to complete in order to find myself
again.
i hope you find solace in reading this as much as
i did while writing it.

heat wave...

heat wave...
across the concrete
watermelon seeds

- free palestine

time of dragons

my belly is swollen with life,
and my mind clouded with the idea
that my very breath breaks after every kick to
the ribs
from societys' expectations
of how to raise a heroine in a time of dragons.
every fiery breath of man I match
with the acid in the back of my throat
as I spit contempt at their boots
when they fail to push me off the hill I so
breathlessly climbed
paving a way for my little warrior.
and she shall know that every aching step,
and every aching fist,
drove me further and further across the
battlefield of
cultists dressed in black robes and powdered
wigs,
striking their giant wooden hammers
at anyone brave enough to deny their rule.
and though some days I'm crawling
on my hands and knees across those fields,
pausing at every gut-wrenching reaction,
I shall gladly shed the blood needed
to smear the campaigns and rallies

so that she does not have to,
for even the biggest,
richest,
and scariest dragons
are no match against
the mothers and women
they tried to burn
so long ago

opening night

The first time I saw her was from behind a curtain. It was like I was watching my own personal Broadway performance and here's the star of the show: my bitsy baby, covered in amniotic fluids and screaming. The next time I open my eyes she's in front of me: clean, wrapped in a swaddle, and wearing a pink beanie the nurses had tied into bunny ears to honor her arrival on Easter Sunday. She's placed on my chest and her lips find my cheek. They say true love's kiss can break any curse—only this time it's from my own blood. She's healed me; she's healed my soul. I don't remember ever feeling my mother's love. Now I'm on the other end and all I can think about is the curl of her hair, her dark eyes, and her soft skin. I want to hold onto her and cover her in kisses in return. The first time I saw her was over a curtain—and the walls around my heart crumbled; the first curse she healed.

cherry blossom petal…
the curve
of her bottom lip

autumn rain

5

autumn rain—
a martyr
in pink pajamas

hay is for horses

The barn still smells the same as it did twenty years ago. It looks different: the stalls are new; there's a pen for lambs on the other side; the grain and oats have moved; there's saddles and stands I've never seen before. And yet, when I slide open that giant metal door, suddenly, I'm eight years old again, surrounded by the bales of hay piled high to the ceiling, emitting a musky, sweet scent. Even the same radio still plays softly in the corner.

The horses in the stalls whiny and snort when the door slides open. I pick up Bitsy and we hold out our hands, palms up. Nostrils twitch and relax. Blink. We're accepted. I scratch the white patch between his big, black eyes. Bitsy places her tiny hand on the bridge of his nose. He watches us, thankful for the love. Bitsy giggles and calls out "Horsey!" before blowing a wet raspberry, spitting dribble down her chin. I set her down. She looks up. The horse looks down at her. She giggles again, undeterred by the gentle giant now standing before her. As I watch, a warming sensation fills my chest as

tears fill my eyes—and a hole in my heart that I
didn't even know was missing in the first place.

childhood farm—
gallop around
my memories

this is for

This is for all the times I have cried myself to sleep. This is for all the times I slept through the pain instead of feeling it. This is for all the times I felt pain and didn't feel safe to feel it. This is for all the times I buried my pain out of fear. This is for all the times I've felt fear and frustration after not being heard. This is for all the times I didn't feel heard and supported. This is for all the times I wasn't supported during my hardships. This is for all the times when not only were my hardships punished, but so were my successes. This is for all the times I succeeded and felt proud just to be scorned or laughed at. This is for all the times I've been scorned or laughed at for enjoying something that didn't fit the status quo. This is for all the times I didn't fit into the status quo and couldn't figure out why. This is for all the times I couldn't figure out why I was so different from everyone else. This is for all the times I felt so different that I cried myself to sleep.

snow day…
a fridge full
of drawings

journal moment #1804: snow

9

"…It sure is beautiful outside... I always loved how the day after a snowstorm looks. It's so calm, and the birds and squirrels emerge from their nests to feast. It's like the forest is in limbo, trying to catch its breath after withstanding such a storm. The whole world is on pause when you step out between the trees, which are covered in snow and ice. I really admire the strength of the trees during these times…Father Winter has no effect on the sturdy, deep-rooted vigor of the tall pines, mighty oaks, and hardy maples…"

first snow…
tiny boots
by the fire

this is why

why
won't
you
just
talk
to
me
each word
enunciated
by the smashing
of his fist
against the bathroom door
the wood splintering
before crashing to the floor
not taking a minute
to think
maybe
this
is
why
I
can't
talk

autumn moon

I fell in love in the middle of a chilly, autumn
night. We spent hours walking along and
laughing on an empty beach. The moon was full
and illuminated the sands, water, and blue hint
of his eyes. The night sky was expansive—every
millimeter of space was sprinkled with glowing,
twinkling stars. The sky was indistinguishable
from the water until just a few feet out from
shore. There, the stars dipped below the horizon
and turned into silver sea-sprites riding the
waves. We rode the magic dragon and quoted
adult cartoons. We shared stories and took turns
apologizing for talking so much. We star-gazed
and talked to the waves. We watched the sprites,
dancing in the moonlight. We fell in love in the
middle of a chilly, autumn night.

autumn moon—
she has
his dimples

thin skin

12

you scratch my arm
and lick the blood from my wound
yet when asked
you deny
and lie
and blame me
for having thin skin

pearl

her skin shone softly
like that of a pearl:
only at the right moment
will you get a glimpse of her colors,
for she too
started as but a grain of sand
growing layer by layer
year after year
until the right moment arrived
and she was set free
forever shimmering
under the gentle glow
of his care

inner critic

I don't have many memories from age five to thirteen. I have snapshots, polaroids hanging out of order by rainbow-colored clothespins on fraying twine tied to pushpins jabbed into my dormroom walls. I don't know how old I am in any of these pictures, nor do I know what year it is. Memory is funny like that. Am I remembering the event for what it was, or am I remembering the last time I remembered that memory? Details are fuzzy. The faces blur. But their voices? They're still clear as day. "Bitch!" snapped the mother's voice. "You got something to say?!" screamed the father's voice. "Next time, don't tell me stop," threatened the boy's voice. "You're not doing it right," complained an abuser. "You're too sensitive," scoffed a boyfriend. "You can't buy that!" controlled the unemployed.

I guess one of the better parts of getting older is making new memories that eventually overpower the old ones.

long night…

the phonograph
skips

flames

she's been surrounded by flames
licking at her heels
and scorching the hem of her dress
for as long as she can remember,
her soles bear callouses
to protect her
against the embers she has tread,
her hands tied by the silence expected of her,
as if she enjoys the stakes
she was unwillingly bound to,
yet over the crackling fire
she remains tall
for these flames mean nothing
compared to the depths of hell
she's already been through,
you can tell by the smile she wears
and the flickering heat reflecting in her eyes
as she stares down the scythe-bearer
holding the gas can

journal moment #2485: inner teen

"…all I wanna do now is cry for my teen self. She went through so much. And got shit on so badly by everyone around her. All she wanted was to be loved. To be accepted. To have friends and fun. To be a normal fucking teenager. She tried so hard. I tried. She is me after all. And now all I can do is grieve for what wasn't, accept that it can't be changed, and give it all to Bitsy…"

autumn wind…
walking past
the whispers

after party…
the cake
still legible

christmas eve

Christmas Eve in a big city convenient store is like a tornado set a bull free in a glitter shop. For five hours, I watched humanity see red over red: ribbons, ornaments, tissue paper, you name it. The gift bag aisle was a land mind, no matter how many times I sent bomb technicians back to clear the way again. Cheap ornaments sold by the handfuls, candy canes by the dozens. Boxes of wrapping paper lined the windows, disrupting our view of a snowy concrete jungle that reflected reds, greens, and yellows from the city street lights. Purchase after purchase. Transaction after transaction. Customer after customer. Did you find everything okay? Would you like gift wrapping? Paper or plastic? Credit card or debit? Would you like to donate a toy to charity? Happy Holidays?

Everyone's mother and grandmother were there, trying to grab a last-minute purchase on their never-ending holiday to-do list. The store happens to be next to a supermarket, then to the post office before it closes. Then gotta get home to cook dinner. Get the kids to bed so the gift wrapping can be done…They were just as

frantic going through the gift bags as I was
watching them. Will this fit? Are gift boxes still
a thing? How big was that one box? Does this
tissue paper match that one bag? Is that enough
wrapping paper? How many feet is 78 inches?
Will blue work instead of green?

A million tiny voices, a million tiny questions,
not a single second to breathe.

after hours—
red glitter
between my toes

meteor shower

meteor showers...
from the river
to the sea

famous?

is this what it's like to be famous?
everyone in this town,
anyone who's anyone knows…
it's cemented in brass
displayed for eternity,
they don't know me though,
no one ever remembers me,
not until I mention my maiden name
or my father's name
or my grandfather's…
is this what it's like to be famous?
everyone recognizes your name,
but they don't actually know you?

withering wind…
the city museum
papa's plaque

armageddon

you once told me
the world doesn't evolve around you
so when he held me down
and his devilish tongue
infiltrated my garden of eden,
how could i tell you
i was in armageddon
when the sun was shining
through their kitchen window,
the rays kissing your feet
while at the same time
burning *whore* into mine

- *childhood confessionals*

journal moment #3985: firsts

"…my parents. My siblings. My grandparents.
Teachers. Friends. Classmates. School.
Summers. Seasons. Pets. Before Ian, I've never
had a single, stable relationship with anything
before. Even our family dogs never made it past
three years old most times. My life now…has
been the most stable it's ever been. Ever. First
home I've lived in consecutively...going on three
years next week. Longest relationship ever with
a human...My life, currently, is the exact
opposite of the one I lived as a child. Only now,
I'm the one in control…things don't just happen
around me and I have to respond to it—I make
things happen. I control the income and the
outcome this time. It's my life, no one else's. I
have the power, ability, knowledge, and love to
do anything I want to do…"

first frost…
totes
of bubble wrap

granny panties

i have a scar that tells me what to wear
i have a scar that warns me not to care
i have a scar seven layers deep
i have a scar that has made me weep
i have a scar in exchange for a deal, and now
i have a scar that changed how I feel:

my body grew life
my body grew love
my body stayed strong
when i'd had enough

so many people
the lights are so white
i shut my eyes
but it's still so bright

my arms splayed out
feeling nailed down
trying not to think
trying not to drown

one hard tug
two
then a WRETCHED shove

"she's here!"
"she's here!"
a chorus from above

ten little fingers
ten tiny toes
two bright eyes
one perfect nose

i have a scar that tells me what to wear
i have a scar that reminds me not to care
i have a scar and i still look like candy
when i get dressed in my granny panties

the love behind the myth

no one knows their story
nor do they bother to understand,
how he was able to see
past the inferno
everyone else tried to snuff out,
and yet he saw
an explosive passion,
consuming justness, and
a burning desire for freedom
from the maternal vines
that entangled her,
and he brought her into
a kingdom of her own,
where he pours her a glass
of pomegranate wine
as she watches her roses
bloom,
wither,
and die
to make a crown of thorns
and stand by his side as queen
of the very darkness she was once
afraid of too

www.ingramcontent.com/pod-product-compliance
Lightning Source LLC
La Vergne TN
LVHW021331200726
843509LV00014B/2483